ALFRISTON VILLAGE SCHOOL
1879 – 1908

W H JOHNSON

DOWNSWAY BOOKS

First published in 1992 by
DOWNSWAY BOOKS
58 Berkeley Court
Wilmington Square
Eastbourne BN21 4DX

Reprinted 2006

Copyright WH Johnson 1992

Typeset by MCM, Alfriston
Printed & bound by
CPI Antony Rowe, Eastbourne

British Library Cataloguing in Publication Data

A catalogue record for this book is available
From the British Library

ISBN 0 9518564 2 1

CONTENTS

Foreword

FOREWORD

Yet another short book about Alfriston? There can be few places of comparable size so frequently written about as this East Sussex village. But deservedly so for it enjoys a matchless setting, snug in a placid river valley and overlooked by the South Downs. The very thought of the place is enough to make the writer reach for his adjectives.

Admittedly there are no great palaces and few really grand residences in the immediate neighbourhood but all around, as well as in the village itself, there are comfortable cottages, substantial houses and attractive old inns. The Church stands on a mound on the village green and from here there are gentle strolls to the sea along the banks of the Cuckmere or more exhilarating walks across smooth-backed downland. If Alfriston is a much-visited village, then little wonder: it is idyllic. Visitors here confess to feeling themselves in the presence of the past.

Nevertheless, despite all of the writing that this undeniably attractive village has prompted, there is little which tells us of its people, nothing which describes the effect of some great national policy upon the place and how ordinary men and women were affected by it. Indeed, ordinary people and their lives have been overlooked by most - although not all - writers who have seemed to see the village only as if it were some handsome but underpeopled stage set. Sometimes we come across a member of an influential family, a shopkeeper, a smuggler or two, or the occasional 'character' but for the most part the village is deserted. It is for this reason that I have written this account, attempting to introduce a larger cast against a background of nationally-inspired local developments.

The four hundred and fifty-seven handwritten pages of the School Log Book and the four volumes of the School Board Minutes, also handwritten, are documents which until now have not been much used for such an account. Yet their entries are of considerable value. They tell us how, day by day, month by month, over thirty years, the Government's policy of full-time, compulsory education for all was being implemented and how the grand purposes of Westminster contrasted with the more mundane events and sometimes less enthusiastic responses in Alfriston. Through the pages of these contemporary sources we are introduced, albeit most often for no more than a sentence length, to some of history's bit-part players.

This is not a definitive work. It describes no more than a sliver of the history of an ancient place. Yet I hope it gives some savour of the time and its people as well as some idea of how, often against the odds, the school at Alfriston progressed in those years when it was sited on the village green.

I have used the spellings of names as they appear in the original documents. In some cases they may be misspelt but I have felt it wiser to leave them as they are. Similarly, I have not tampered with punctuation.

My thanks are due to Miss Jo Jenner, former head teacher of Alfriston County Primary School and to the present head teacher, Mrs Sandra Mitchell, both of whom have been cooperative in this venture. I am also grateful to David Summerfield for his crisp observations on the first draft.

I should like to express my gratitude to the Museum of the History of Education at the University of Leeds and especially to Mrs Gillian Walker, the Clerk to the Museum, who sent me the examples of text books and of children's work which appear in this booklet.

My greatest debts are to the successive Masters at Alfriston School, Mr W T Brown, Mr E J Dance, Mr H B Greey, Mr W Pinyoun and their colleagues and, of course, to the hundreds of boys and girls who attended the school on the Tye in the years from 1879 to 1908. Nor must I neglect mention of Mr C H Pagden, Clerk to the School Board for so many of those years. I hope that my selection of material does not misrepresent any of them.

1. THE SCHOOL ON THE TYE 1879 - 1908

The principal building on the Tye, Alfriston's village green, is St Andrew's Church. Next to it stands what is today a fine-looking house to which is attached the single-storey War Memorial Hall. At one time the house, built in 1844, served as the Master's quarters and the long low building, which goes back to 1817, as his school.

In 1821 the National Society for the Promotion of Education of the Poor in the Principles of the Established Church opened a school on the premises. The education offered by this National School was part-time, voluntary and free. The Trustee of the building was the Vicar of Alfriston. The teaching was undertaken by either the clergy or their appointees. Then in 1878, as a consequence of national legislation, School Boards were elected throughout the country. Their task was to oversee a system of compulsory full-time education for all children up to the age of ten, which was to be paid for by those attending. So it was that for an annual rent of two guineas (£2.10) paid to the Church, the Alfriston School Board took over both house and building. The new system of state education was to be established in the village and to serve the surrounding parishes of Milton Street, Lullington, Litlington and the Contributory District of Arlington.

In this brief account of Alfriston School I have attempted to offer an example of the awkward beginnings of compulsory education. Imagine across this country, cities and towns coping with this daunting task; imagine, too, the rural backwaters proffering their own brand of enlightenment to not totally grateful communities. Picture this village, Alfriston, shorn of its present-day tea-rooms and souvenir shops, of its coaches disgorging visitors daily, of its large number of retired incomers and non-manual workers. A hundred and twenty years ago this was a working village, a farming community, now beginning to feel the effects of agricultural decline. Rural poverty was on the increase throughout the country. The comfortable Alfriston of today did not exist; the myth of Merrie England, or at least the nostalgia for it that it now sometimes projects, had not yet developed. And it was precisely then that the Government thought it appropriate to

1

introduce compulsory, paid-for schooling. It might reduce crime, some said; it might lead to a brighter future; we might be able to maintain our economic position against other countries, particularly the newly united and powerful Germany. The three R's would provide a better educated work force, they said, in the way that today we make the same remarks about technological and computer education. In consequence from 1879 all five year olds were expected to go to school and stay there until they were at least ten years old.

So what of this first generation of full-time pupils? How did they respond to it? What did their parents feel about it? Did they hope it offered a key to new freedoms? Did they harbour new ambitions? Some did.

Perhaps the Weekes family up at Winton Street - there were ten children - felt some pride when Fanny was appointed pupil teacher. And surely School Board member Ebenezer Comfort, draper and grocer too - his shop is now the village post office - experienced a glow when three of his children in turn became monitors and later pupil teachers. And then, did not his son Jesse actually become a full-blown Assistant Teacher at the school? And Davies Dumbrell? Did he not chuckle to himself when in 1895 his daughter Eunice told the Board she would stay on as pupil teacher only if her weekly wage went up to three shillings?

Of course, there were disappointments. How upset churchwarden and shopkeeper Mr Doble must have been when young Frederick, who had been doing so well as pupil teacher, was refused permission to continue in his work by the Board of Education on account of his lameness. No matter how the School Board and the Master pleaded on Frederick's behalf, those up in London were adamant.

And there are other families. The Marchants of the High Street and those of Litlington, the Levetts, the Bakers and the Lelliotts figure in the Log Book written by successive Masters and in the Minute Books of the School Board. There are the Hiltons and Burgesses, Herriotts and Normans, Woods and Walkers. These handwritten records tell some of Alfriston's story, some of England's. There is poor Mrs Cottrell, not so much complaining about the school fee but saying it should at least be equitable. Mrs Carter struggles with the fees for her six children: her husband earns fourteen shillings a week. Mrs Russell asks that the fees be remitted: her husband earns only twelve shillings.

What a problem the fees are. They are raised, lowered, remitted and finally abandoned. What an imposition they are. At a time when the combination of corn growing and sheep rearing is no longer profitable, when work on the land is hard to come by, the powers-that-be not only insist on boys and girls going to school rather than out to work: they even insist on a charge. All previous centuries had seen Alfriston's and England's young out gleaning, bird scaring, stone picking, weeding, harvesting, doing any of the multitudinous tasks required of a largely machineless agricultural economy. When the Lowers and the Kemps and so many others stayed away from school, who could blame them? Some children said that if by the age of twelve they were not at work they felt guilty.

It is not surprising that there were parents who resisted paying fees: small wonder they wanted no truck with this business of seemingly endless schooling. How much does a boy or girl have to know? people asked. Must they be forever at their desks? After all, if they had not mastered their ABCs and their 1, 2, 3s by the time they were eight or nine, then they never would. Why keep them in school?

It was not as if people were totally opposed to learning. School was fine as far as it went. Indeed, several local parents in the 1860s and 1870s sent their children either to Miss Winch's private school or to the National School. There is nevertheless a seeming curiosity here. Some, sent to these schools at four or five years of age were later, when attendance became compulsory, sometimes brought before the magistrates for non-attendance. Perhaps the answer is that it was better to send small children off to school, out of dark, cramped, crowded cottages where they were forever under everyone's feet. Once they were old enough for field work, however, or able to carry meals to labouring fathers, then school was over.

But once the system is in place, the Log Book tells us of many children trudging through snow, fog, ice, mud, of their having difficulties in reaching school or home because of floods. On dark winter days they go to and fro, with their storm lanterns or their candles in jars. They come over from Lullington or Milton Street, these landless labourers' and small tradesmen's boys and girls, from their often cheerless homes, in their hand-me-down garments, with their worn-out boots, with sacks for protection over their heads and shoulders. They sit in their crowded schoolroom - perhaps ninety of them in the big room and may be forty in the infants' - with their wet clothing ranged round the Tortoise stove throughout the day. But think of the days when it is not the time of year for fires or when the stove is not working; think of the soaked-through infants in their gallery seats and the older boys and girls shivering in their cramped six-seater Windsor desks. At midday, before going out to play on the Tye, they take out their bread and cheese and drink their bottles of cold tea or their mugs of water from the well in the Master's garden. They face the afternoon and then for many there is the long trudge home. If the floods are up they will have to cross the river by Sherman's Bridge on the present A27 if they are to reach Milton Street or other places on that side of the water.

From 1879 until 1908, there were four Masters. Two, Messrs Brown and Dance, between them stayed only for the first fourteen months. But their observations are interesting. For the rest of the time, Mr Greey stayed for eight years whilst his successor Mr Pinyoun was Master for twenty years.

In the Log Book the Masters tell of their frustrations; they complain of the stench from the 'offices' - what a saga the 'offices' are to be. They tell of the Board's refusal to allow lights in school with the consequence that work cannot continue on dark winter afternoons; they write about visits from the Vicar and members of the Board and of Mr Bodle's deliveries of chloride of lime for the 'offices', black lead and soap and other necessities. They are irritated by the path across the Tye: it is a quagmire. One Master fully understands parents' reluctance to send children through such mud. But then the Tye was often under water: in those days and indeed until the 1930s, there were no retaining banks to hold back the Cuckmere when it was in flood.

All the illnesses - the measles, whooping cough, scarlet fever, typhoid fever, diphtheric throats, 'breaking out', ringworm, chicken pox - some of which led to long school closures, are recorded here. And yet, mercifully, and in spite of all we are led to expect of the time, in thirty years only three pupil deaths are recorded.

These Masters admonish recalcitrant parents; they complain that pupils' education has no continuity, hindered as it is by illness and by parents encouraging their children to do field work; they ask they ask that those responsible should not arrange 'treats' and outings in school time; they despair at the constant changes of Assistant Teachers, usually young ladies who spend only a term or two before moving on elsewhere.

I can find only two references to punishment in the Log Book. On one occasion three pupils are detained until 5pm for truancy. Did they practise handwriting in their copy books? Or 'long tots' in their arithmetic books? Did they sit in total silence? Or perhaps weed the Master's garden?

Elsewhere, we read:

"11th June 1888 I, William Pinyoun, Certificated Master, take charge of the school today.
18th June 1888. Gave Albert Taylor and Fred Walker each one stroke of the cane for continued disobedience."

The new man has made his mark.

I cannot trace a Punishment Book although I do not believe that there never was one. Although one of the Inspectors' reports states that the children are wisely and kindly treated, I am unable to bring myself to think that these late Victorian and Edwardian gentlemen were so in advance of their time and so alien to their period that they did not physically punish both boys and girls with some regularity.

Elsewhere, the documents reveal the conditions of the buildings. They are bad when the School Board takes them over from the National School and they are bad right through. Year after year, the Masters complain of their shortcomings. So too do Her Majesty's Inspectors of Schools in their annual Reports. In the end, there is no alternative to a new building and in 1908 the school moves to its present site in North Road.

For the Masters and pupils there is the constant anxiety about the annual report by the Inspectors. On their judgement depends the amount of Grant paid to the school. If the children do well - and they are often over-awed by these grand former public school men who have themselves rarely taught - the Grant, out of which will come part of the Master's salary, will be good. But if the children forget the lessons they have been drilled in, the Grant will be less good. And then what will the Board say? Later, the

Grant depended upon attendance. The Board was then equally anxious for good attendance: lower Grant always meant higher rates.

Not that the Board Members expected too much in the way of learning. The Code of Standards, described later in this booklet, is evidence of that. The framers of the various Education Acts had no great ambitions for those in receipt of elementary education. True enough, the supercilious Robert Lowe had announced to the House of Commons that "We must prevail upon our future masters to learn their letters" but neither he nor the Government of the day had any intention that any child in a state school should undergo a liberal and liberating experience. And whilst they would like an efficient system, they would favour even more one which was cheap.

The Code of Standards did at its worst encourage an education which too often offered to pupils an irreducible minimum of learning. Sometimes, though not always, visiting Inspectors described the pupils as unintelligent or slow: it is more likely that the undemanding and limiting nature of some of the work failed to release the intellectual energy and ability of very many children. The Victorian Code of Standards expected little of the children of the poor: not infrequently the children lived down to those expectations.

In August 1880 the Eastbourne Board of Guardians of the Poor felt constrained to write to G B Gregory, the local MP. These powerful men indicated clearly enough what the Board schools should be doing. "Education of the Children of the Poor" should be, they wrote, "only in such branches of useful knowledge as is necessary to fit them to earn their bread intelligently and suitably to their position." Thus, the position of the children of the poor was ordained to be at the bottom of the pile. The Guardians were, of course, speaking as men of their class, position, and time. Some of them, such as Spencer Austen Leigh of Frog Firle House, the Reverend Hedges, Messrs Ade, Richardson and Hewett, were members of the Alfriston United School Board. The boundaries of learning in rural schools were demarcated by such men of influence, wealthy landowners, substantial tenant farmers, as well as well-meaning drapers like Comfort and earnest builders such as John Wilson. These men wanted no frills in education. This was not secondary education: it was elementary education and it was on the rates. There were to be no fanciful features, no mathematics, no sciences, no foreign languages. Such elements, the Guardians told Mr Gregory were "injurious to the essential ground work of all Education: reality, accuracy and thoroughness".

How precisely Dickens has these people in mind when he writes in 'Hard Times':

"You are to be in all things regulated and governed," said the gentleman, "by fact. We hope to have before long, a board of fact, composed of commissioners of fact, who will force the people to be a people of fact. You must discard the word Fancy altogether."

Yet according to their lights, the members were loyal to Alfriston Board School. They took their tasks seriously. Two of them - Spencer Austen Leigh and Ebenezer Comfort - attended the first meeting in 1878 and were there right to the dissolution of the Board in 1903 when the school was taken over by the County Council. C H Pagden served in the capacity of clerk throughout this period.

In spite of all difficulties, the school prospered. Numbers on roll grew from seventy-three to a hundred and sixty and the hall, partitioned in two, must very frequently have been decidedly crowded in both infant and mixed school sections. But this was not unusual in schools at this period. Such large and crowded classes did, of course, tend to impose a teaching style in which a narrow rigidity was already encouraged by the Code of Standards. Nevertheless, the evidence of the Log Book does suggest that even these inhibiting elements did not wholly prevent the broadening of the curriculum as the years went by.

Pages 9 to 11

Head Teachers are still required to maintain a record of matters of significance to the school. The following pages contain typical entries made by Mr Brown (1879), Mr Greey (1886), and Mr Pinyoun (1908).

8

Febry. 10th This school, formerly in connection with the
National Society, opens to-day under the man-
agement of the Alfriston United District School
Board, having been closed since July 26. 1878.
I commenced duties as Master on the same
day, being assisted by Miss K. E. Brown.

- 14th Rev. J. J. Hedges, Vicar of Alfriston, Chairman, &
Mr. C. H. Pagden, Clerk, to the School Board,
visited the School on Monday (10th)
Examined the various standards & found them
all in an extremely backward condition: Stan I
especially so. Majority of Stan IV unable to do
work of Stan II in Arithmetic.
Admitted 54 children during week. Average 48.6.
Several children entirely cut off from School by
the floods for two or three days.

- 21st Admitted 17 children on Mon. (17th) & one on Tuesday.
Weather still very wet & floods but slightly abated.
Unable to work at present by any definite Time
Table owing to unsatisfactory state of Standards.
The week has been occupied in back work as
no standard is at present able to go on with its
own particular work.

from the well in front of the house, for analysis —

May 26th Received a note from Mrs Boys, Hobbs Hoath, stating that her children were suffering from colds & coughs, and thereby not able to attend school.

" 28th The attendance of the children, particularly the girls, of the upper division of the school, is anything but that which is desired. 16 are absent to-day; 49 on the books. Average for the week - 110·8.
" " past month. 118·4
" " " Quarter 108·

May 31st Admitted Frederick Hilton
Ruth Walker too late to be marked present.

June 1st Geo & Charley Crouch too late to be marked present in the morning.
The family of Lelliotts from Lullington are unable to attend this week from illness

" 4th Several children absent this week at work for Mr Burton.
Average 110·8. No on books - 134

a Rehearsal of the Pevensey Pageant at Pevensey.

July 20th | Rose Pickard pupil-teacher absent all day.

" 24. | Very good attendance during past week.

29 | Received large parcel of goods in respect of estimate sent in 5th April last. As these goods have been so long delayed I have found it impossible to satisfactorily complete the re-examination at end of this term

31. | Closed school for Summer Vacation. Alice Taylor resigned her post as monitress in Infants' Div:

2. THE CURRICULUM

What children were to learn was laid down in the Code of Standards. There was in consequence a strong temptation to teach the boys and girls no more than was required in the Code. As long as the basics were right when the Inspectors called, the Grant was paid. After what must have been quite cursory tests, judgements were arrived at and payment made in accordance with the results. The effect of this procedure was learning by rote, copying directly from the blackboard, parrotting one or two poems, reading simple passages over and over again, chanting tables and constant testing. It was unadventurous; it was probably dull and perhaps this is why, from time to time, teachers felt obliged to introduce new material. The content of the curriculum did expand, did become more challenging during the period described in this account.

There is no clear indication of the timetable followed at the school but scripture and prayers took between half an hour and an hour each day. The bulk of the time was devoted to the three R's. Singing was important as were drawing and needlework both of which attracted Grant money. There were occasions when needlework was temporarily abandoned at Alfriston Board School but it was a socially important subject for girls who for the most part would go into service and who would need to be able at least to tack, hem and gather and make simple garments.

Reading books were chosen for their moral content and often contained no more than a series of unconnected extracts of stories simply told. There was a greater emphasis upon the mechanics of reading than upon the story. Penmanship was important, there being constant handwriting practice in copy books. The results were often excellent.

Object lessons appear frequently in the curriculum. These were the children's basic introductions to natural history, botany, biology and general science.

Geography and history were also placed on the teaching programme. Geography was usually concerned with the location of towns and countries; history with the reigns of the Kings and Queens of England.

Any detailed study of literature, poetry, drama, languages and mathematics and sciences were, however, relegated to the realms of Fancy as Dickens had foretold. These were reserved for secondary schools. Nevertheless, what was on offer in curriculum terms in 1908 was distinctly richer than the original thin offering of 1879.

The Diocesan Authorities continued to visit the school to examine Scripture.

The following extracts illustrate much of the above.

14th February 1879   Examined the various standards and found them all in an extremely backward condition: Standard I especially so. Majority of Standard IV unable to do work of Standard II in Arithmetic.

7th March 1881   Miss Greey has long since given up the idea of taking needlework as a class subject, having found the girls very backward in this subject of instruction.

11th July 1881   Commenced reduction of weights and measures with the 4th Standard this week.

23rd September 1881   Commenced Subtraction with 1st Standard and Proportion in the 5th.

17th January 1883   The occasion of the Examination in Divinity by the Rev. R. Blight. The children obtained 30 certificates, 10 of which were excellent.

17th September 1883   The following is a List of Object Lessons given during the Year - Lion, Duck, Fox, Dog, Bread, Coal, Pig, Leaves, Heat, Seasons, Rainbow, Cat, Bees, Mouse, Horse, Plough, Cheese, Birds Nests, Light, Cow, Clouds, Spade, Iron, Hen, Wind, Turkey, Camel, Knife.

15th October 1883	Received of the National Society pictures of Horse, Camel, Cat, Sheep.
9th March 1886	William Lelliott and Henry Hilton being unfit to proceed to a Standard above will continue to work in the Second.
27th April 1888	Geography will not be taken with the Girls this year; the time formerly given to it will be devoted to Needlework.
23rd July 1888	Commenced a series of exercises in School Drill.

27th March 1892	Work for 1892 - 1893
	Poetry Standard
	I What Came of Firing a Gun
	II The Dog at His Master's Grave
	III The Ploughshares of Old England
	   and How Cheery are the Marines
	IV - VII Lochiel's Warning
	   and The Battle of the Baltic

Except where indicated, the following are extracts from annual reports by Her Majesty's Inspectors.

23rd April 1883	The percentage of passes in Elementary subjects is nearly 91. Last year it was nearly 87. The Arithmetic was well done. The Children passed with credit in Geography. The Needlework is about fair. The Singing is nice.

22 February 1884	School inspected on January 18th, 1884.
	   Old Testament - Very Good
	   New Testament - Very Good
	   Elementary Christian Doctrine - Good
	   Repetition - Good

The School is becoming a large and important one admirably conducted by Mr Greey.

The Singing of Hymns is very good.

Robert Blight, Diocesan Inspector

28th March 1884   The children are rather slow to answer questions. They should be encouraged to speak out when they answer and when they read. The Girls were backward in Mental Arithmetic. The English earns the fair grant. The Geography earns the good one. The Good Merit Grant is recommended with pleasure.

Amount of Grant £71. 18. 6.

25th April 1884   The Girls must do their Examination Sewing pieces better next time to secure the payment of the good grant.

21st April 1885   The Teachers deserve praise for what they have done.

31st January 1887   Repetition of passages of Holy Scripture is accurate.

Walter Walsh, Diocesan Inspector

27th April 1888   The highest Merit Grant is again recommended but with hesitation and there should be an improvement in the oral work if this mark is to be improved.

12th April 1889   In the First and Second Standards the hemming stitches are unnecessarily small ... in the Fourth and Fifth Standards the darning needs attention.

29th April 1892   The habit of whispering and random answering to oral question has not been eradicated.

		25th March 1893	The Excellent Grant has been awarded.

25th March 1893   The Excellent Grant has been awarded.

Report of Drawing Examiner

9th April 1893   Recitation and Geography are fairly good so is Reading except from the point of intelligence. English barely deserves a Grant.

20th April 1896   Girls do not answer so well as the Boys in Geography. Children were disposed to talk and be inattentive during the Dictation Lesson.

The Infants are bright, intelligent children and appear happy and interested in their work.

2nd April 1897   <u>Mixed School</u> Mr Pinyoun is a careful and painstaking teacher and what I saw of the work on my visits was well or fairly well done.

<u>Infants</u> The efficiency of the Infants class has been well maintained.

This report is followed by the Grant calculation which is largely based on attendance.

	Mixed School	Infants
Average attendance	<u>83</u>	<u>38</u>
Grant	12/6	9/-
" (Variable)	1/-	6/-
" (Drawing and Needlework)	-	1/-
" (Singing)	1/-	1/-
" (Geography)	2/-	-
	16/6	17/-

Grant (Mixed School)	£ 68. 9. 6.
Grant (Needlework)	£ 4. 4. 0.
Grant (Infants)	£ 32. 6. 0.

£104. 19. 6

15th April 1899	At my first visit the first Standard only did twenty minutes Reading instead of the forty allotted in the timetable and the Second Standard only did ten minutes instead of twenty. Neither then nor at my second visit was I able to assign a good mark for this important subject.
	The work generally and discipline appear to be as in former years. A great deal of talking goes on in the Mixed School. The Infants are properly taught.

The place of Scripture in the curriculum had been assured in the Education Act. Its place was unassailable. In all schools, in addition to an act of worship, there was a daily Scripture lesson. Only an event of almost unimaginable significance could interfere with this regime. When one day Mr Pinyoun abandoned this daily requirement, he recorded it in the Log Book.

23rd January 1901	Informed the children of the death of our Queen; and, in place of the usual Scripture lesson, gave a lesson appropriate to the sad event.

In the new century, the Inspectors were often encouraging in their reports.

15th April 1901	... another meritorious year's work in spite of drawbacks, some preventable and others avoidable. The Sewing deserves a word of praise and Discipline is better than it was.

17

26th January 1903   Mr Pinyoun as usual is working well in the Upper School but he is overweighted with the charge of the Third to the Seventh Standards inclusive.

12th May 1905   The Children are kindly and wisely treated and are encouraged to use their eyes. There is an evident desire to adopt fresh ideas. The elder boys showed some capital sketches in their Nature notebooks.

26th January 1907   ... the first year's attempt at Nature Study is very commendable.

'Reading without Tears' is typical of its time. If it was not used at the local school, children would learn to read from a similar book.

The passage entitled 'The Washing Day' comes from 'The Advanced Excelsior Book V'. It was intended to be entertaining and instructive.

The maxims at the foot of the page were meant to have some improving effect. 'The Black Prince' is from the same book. Jingoistic poems of this kind remained popular well into the Twentieth Century.

Bag Bat Bab

Bag Bat Bab

bag bat bab

NOTE.—The Child should call the first consonant by its sound (not by its name), and he should not divide the two other letters, but say B'—ag, Bag.

Man Mat Map

Man Mat Map

man mat map

NOTE.—The Teacher is recommended to print on Cards the words in these and the following pages, and to ask the Child to place these little cards on the Pictures.

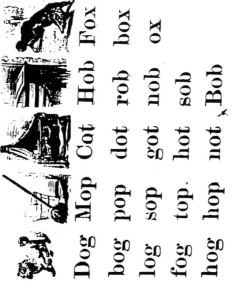

Dog Mop Cot Hob Fox

bog pop dot rob box

log sop got nob ox

fog top. hot sob

hog hop not Bob

Bob has got a box

Bob has got a fox

Bob has got a cot

Bob has got a hog

Bob has got a dog

Bob has got a top

Bob has got hot sop

Bob is not in the fog

Bob is in his cot

Did Bob sob in his cot

Bob did sob. Jog the cot

My top is in my box

My sop is on the hob

know	wrong	lamb
knew	wrap	thumb
knit	write	limb
knock	wrote	debt
knot	wren	clothes
knife		
knave	knuckle	wreath	high
knead	gnat	wrist	though
knee	gnash	wretch	dough
kneel	gnaw	wrench	psalm

Molly milks the cow.

Roger drives the plough.

Sam can reap and mow.

Sal can knead the dough.

Tom was riding and fell off.

Bab was choking with a cough.

Dick will stuff with paste and puff.

But Harry knows he's had enough.

Lucy wears her little muff

When-e'er the wind is sharp and rough.

A knave is a de-ceit-ful man

A wretch is a sorrow-ful man.

A wren is the small-est of English birds.

The joints of the limbs are very use-ful.

The ankles and knees help us to walk.

The wrists and knuckles help us to handle.

There are twelve months in the year.

In Jan-u-ary—boys make snow-balls.

In Feb-ru-ary—girls pluck snow-drops.

In March—high winds blow.

In A-pril—soft showers fall.

In May—hed-ges are cover-ed with blossoms.

In June—gar-dens are fill-ed with flowers.

In Ju-ly—reap-ers cut the corn.

In Au-gust—glean-ers pick up the ears.

In Sep-tem-ber—chil-dren eat black-berries.

In Oc-to-ber—cot-ta-gers gather apples.

In No-vem-ber—fogs cloud the air.

In De-cem-ber—the trees are bare.

the sun; a floury sediment is found at the bottom of the water, this is removed and dried in an oven, and is called starch.

Soap is a mixture of soda and tallow, prepared by boiling.

"There, Mildred," said Bessie, "my book is getting quite valuable to me. What a pity it is, though, that we cannot do without washing altogether. I do not mind washing days, but poor mother always looks so tired."

"It is not the pleasantest sort of work, dear; but it cannot be done without."

"I wonder, Mildred, some people don't invent something to make washing easy; they are always inventing something."

"So there are, Bessie, many things invented—washing secrets, washing powders, and washing machines. My mistress told me that once a Mr. Twelvetrees' professed to have discovered the secret of getting a six weeks' wash done before breakfast, without any rubbing at all; but we don't hear much of it now. I have seen several kinds of washing machines which are a great saving of labour. The chief business is then to turn a wheel, to put in the clothes and water, and to take them out again. The work is so quickly done, that in ten minutes you can wash eight shirts; but they are generally expensive."

"Mildred, I'll save my money and buy one for mother."

QUESTIONS.—How did Bessie help her mother early in the morning on washing day? Why? How many stages should the clothes go through? What should be done in the firsting? . . . in the seconding? . . . the boiling? and the rinsing? Why did Bessie's mother not use washing powders? What sort of water should be used for washing? How should hard water be first treated? What is soda, blue, starch, and soap? What did Mildred say she would buy for her mother? Why is a washing machine useful?

MAXIMS, ETC.

Eat to live, but do not live to eat.

A bad day never hath a good night.

Crosses are ladders that lead up to heaven.

It is not the gay coat makes the gentleman.

Fine dressing is a foul house swept before the windows.

Corn is cleansed with the wind, and the soul with chastening.

THE BLACK PRINCE.*

the Black Prince. See page 75.

Ed'-ward III. See page 73.

Poic-ti-ers', *pr. n.*, a town in Poitou. The battle was fought on Monday September 19, 1356. The town is also noted for the defeat of the Saracens in the neighbourhood, A.D. 732, by Charles Martel.

King John of France ascended the French throne in 1350, and died in England 1364.

Ro'-man cap'-tives. The prisoners war captured by the armies of ancient Rome were sometimes massacred in cold blood. But generally they were reserved for a worse fate. After being carried to Rome, they had to march in chains before the triumphal car of their conqueror through the streets of the city. On reaching the Capitoline hill, the captive chiefs were in many cases taken aside and put to death, while the mass of the captives, who often were at least the equals of their conquerors in education and refinement, were reduced to slavery.

I'LL tell you a tale of a ·knight, my boy,
  The bravest that ever was known :
A lion he was in the fight, my boy,
  A lamb when the battle was done.
Oh, he need not be named; for who has not heard
Of the glorious son of King Edward the Third ?·

Armour he wore as black as jet ;
  His sword was keen and good ;
He conquer'd every ·foe he met,
  And he spar'd them when ·subdued.
Valiant and generous, gentle and bold,
Was, the Black Prince of England in days of old.

Often he charged with spear and lance
  At the head of his ·valorous knights ;
But the battle of Poictiers,* won in France,
  Was the noblest of all his fights :
And every British heart should be
Proud when it thinks of that victory.

The French were many, the English few ;
  But the Black Prince little heeded :
His knights, he knew, were brave and true ;
  Their arms were all he needed.
He ask'd not *how many* might be the foe ;
Where are they? was all that he sought to know.

3. ATTENDANCE

Despite the best efforts of Masters and Attendance Officers - the 'School Board Men' - attendance presented a constant problem. This was not confined to Alfriston: irregular attendance was a matter of national concern. The following extracts will indicate how serious this was locally. Naturally, one cause was sickness.

28th March 1879   Bronchitis seems prevalent.

4th April 1879   One girl, Louisa Cole, was taken on Tuesday with scarlatina.

2nd May 1879   Louisa Cole died on Tuesday, April 29th, after a month's illness, augmented just before her death by taking cold.

16th May 1879   Measles seems very prevalent in the village.

25th July 1879   Several children away with an attack of blister pox.

25th June 1880   Measles are raging in the village.

13th March 1882   The Russells from Winton Street away this morning, Thomas being down with Typhoid Fever.

12th December 1884   ....an epidemic of mumps in the village.

5th January 1885   Mrs Reed's 4 children away from school with Chicken Pox.

11th January 1885   Agnes Richardson, Caroline Burton were sent home today, Ringworm having been discovered on them.

23rd July 1886	.... School closed on account of a severe epidemic of Whooping Cough in the district on June 29th, 1886; and reopened on July 19th, 1886.
7th November 1887	Several children are absent this morning from illness among whom may be mentioned - Maud, Ernest and Minnie Whymark, Kate and Wm Norman, Alice Gatland, Arthur Cole, Charley Pettitt, Ellen Marchant, Ruth Russell, and Edith Teague. The illness consists of a "breaking out" upon the face and head.
2nd January 1888	Harry Pettitt, an Infant, died today.
10th February 1888	Mary Lelliott, Lilian Westgate, Fred Weekes, Harry Westgate, Walter Comfort, Bertha Holton, Rose Bridger, were all absent today, the majority suffering from sore throats.
23rd March 1888	There is a great deal of illness among the children, five or six being unable to walk owing to broken chilblains on the feet.
28th July 1888	The Board decided to close the School for one month on account of measles.
25th August 1888	The Board have decided that the School should remain closed for a further month.
5th November 1888	School reopened after having been closed three weeks (measles).
27th October 1890	The following children are still away on account of scarlet fever - William and Mary Turner; William, Caroline, Ruth, Emily and Louisa Nye; Fred Hilton; Arth. Peters; William, Fred, George and Charles Burgess; Alice and Annie Peters; Harry Nye.

2nd February 1891   Reopened School after having been closed for six weeks. Scarlet Fever has been prevalent in the District since the end of July last.

The members of the School Board and the Vicar, The Reverend F W Beynon, did not enjoy good relations. Unfortunately, his wife too was at loggerheads with the Board on the matter of attendance and illness as the following entries from the Board's Minute Book show.

At the meeting of the Board on 29th July 1892 it was "Resolved that the clerk do communicate with Mrs. Beynon to the effect that it has come to the notice of the School Board that during the last 5 weeks the attendance at the School has fallen off to a degree that causes considerable loss to the ratepayers as the Government Grant will be greatly reduced by it. The Board are aware that this was owing to action taken by her, no doubt under a mistake, reporting that the School was in an unhealthy state and that the School Board bring this matter before her in the hope that the thing will not occur again."

Mrs Beynon replies in somewhat acerbic terms. So much for retiring Victorian ladies.

Alfriston Vicarage
Berwick
Sussex
August 1st '92

Sir,

.... Had the Board been aware that from the end of May to the middle of July, there were at least 20 and 30 cases of scarlet fever and diphtheric throats in the Parish and the immediate neighbourhood, they would hardly have committed the palpable injustice and absurdity of laying to the charge of any one individual the falling off in the attendance of the school. In the judgement of those best qualified to form an opinion, the school should have been closed. Should I at any time deem it expedient to make any complaint in reference to this School I shall lay it before a higher Authority than that of the School Board in Alfriston.

I am, Sir,
Yours truly
(Mrs) C. Crewe Beynon

Mrs Beynon does not indicate precisely to which higher Authority she may refer any future complaint.

24th November 1899   On account of cases of measles in the family, the following children are not attending school - Harmans (3), Taylors (3), Dora Boyles, and Geo. Eldrington. These cases are all from Litlington.

24th October 1900   School closed on account of Whooping Cough.

1st June 1906   There is a great deal of sickness among the children.

Head lice were a problem. Children were not infrequently sent home to have their heads cleaned. John Wilson made a stand, refusing to send his children to school. He was asked for an explanation.

24th July 1884   Mr John Wilson attended the Board and complained that his children frequently during the past three weeks had come home full of vermin. Resolved that the Master be instructed to be as particular as he can be with the children to prevent their being covered with vermin.

(School Board Minute Book)

If sickness was one cause of non-attendance, there were others. In the days before statutory holidays, there had always been occasional celebrations which everyone in the community, young and old, attended. Now, of course, these cut across the School's requirements. This may be the point to say that the major school holiday was usually called the Harvest Holiday and its dates depended upon the readiness of the harvest. The school often began the Harvest Holiday in August. It is noteworthy that no treats took place in this month.

29th October 1879	Chapel School Tea. Only 52 children present.
28th July 1880	Very poor attendance today, owing to a picnic, given by the Tradesmen to the children in the village.
2nd May 1881	Attendance poor this morning, a number of children carrying May poles around.
5th May 1881	Attendance very bad this afternoon owing to a Club Feast at Milton Street.
26th May 1881	Whole holiday this day, it being the Anniversary of the Alfriston Benefit Club.
14th June 1881	Bad attendance this afternoon, owing to the Anniversary of the Congregational Chapel being held.
11th July 1881	Bad attendance caused by a picnic given to the inhabitants.
5th October 1881	... dismissed at 1pm, the occasion of the Sunday School treat.
30th June 1882	Holiday today on the occasion of a picnic of the village people to the sea.
6th February 1884	... dismissed at 11, there being a Meet of the Foxhounds in the village.
26th November 1884	Small attendance a.m. owing to an excursion of the choir children to Brighton.
3rd April 1884	Attendance very poor today owing a great deal to its being Bank Holiday.
21st June 1887	Holiday today it being the occasion of Her Majesty's Jubilee.

10th October 1889	Several children absent on account of the Sale of Farm Stock at Litlington.
27th June 1895	A Holiday given today on account of the annual Fete in connection with the Friendly Societies.
11th July 1895	The usual half holiday given on account of the Chapel Sunday School Treat. I have pointed out to those responsible for the organisation of the Treats that it would be of benefit to the School if it were arranged for them to take place during the Summer Holidays.
25th June 1897	The School has been closed throughout the week, a holiday having been given in celebration of the Queen's Diamond Jubilee.
16th July 1901	Owing to a performance for children in a Circus pitched on the Tye it was impossible to have afternoon school.
10th July 1907	This being one of the days fixed by the Managers for School Treats, the children were taken to Cuckmere Harbour at the invitation of Mr Batho.

The weather contributed greatly to poor attendance as the following extracts show. It was on many more occasions than illustrated here impossible for children to reach school.

14th July 1875	Cut off 2 days - floods.
28th November 1881	Children are prevented from attending school from Litlington, Lullington, and Milton Street, owing to the severe floods.

12th March 1883	The Litlington, Lullington and Milton Street children unable to get to School today on account of Floods.
10th March 1891	A very heavy fall of snow today. Telegram received from Her Majesty's Inspector:- 'No likelihood of getting to Alfriston on Thursday. Another appointment will be made later.'
15th November 1894	The floods throughout the week have been very great. The children have however attended in a praiseworthy manner especially those from Milton Street, a boat having been used to carry them over the water.
5th February 1901	In consequence of the heavy fall of snow, there were less than 13 children present.

Then there was the refusal on the part of some parents to send children to school when work was available. Local farmers were of course greatly annoyed at the inconvenience caused by the insistence of the authorities that children go to school.

8th March 1880	Edward Reed and John Marchant have left for work, being employed by members of the School Board, though neither of them is at present 10 years of age.
15th March 1880	W Marchant (9) gone to work for Mr Brown ... A Kemp gone to work for Mr Levett, a member of the School Board.
23rd April, 1880	John Marchant and Mary Stickley at work, although not eligible.
30th August 1880	Several children absent gleaning.

1st March 1881	Edward Reed and Charles Baker at work, not eligible.
29th July 1881	Average attendance decreasing as Harvest progresses.
20th March 1882	Received a message from Mr Herriott this morning, saying that it was his intention not to send his children to school again.
3rd April 1882	3 boys, John Townsend, Fred Walker and John Burgess, although they failed to satisfy the requirements of the Government at the late examination are being employed.
24th July 1882	Edward Walker has gone to work this morning for Mr Gade although ineligible... The Parent has sent word that she received permission from Mr Hedges (the vicar) to send the boy to work, but on making enquiries this has proved to be false.
4th March 1884	Wrote notes to Messrs Marchant, Olive, Godden, Russell, Cole, Walker, Parsons, Hilton, Reed and Norman with regard to the irregular attendance of their children.
21st July 1884	I am given to understand by Agnes Richardson that her brother has gone to work for Mr Burton.
3rd August 1884	A few of the elder children have gone to work in the harvest fields with their parents. 39 absent.
11th April 1884	Five children are away hop-picking.
16th August 1885	Fred and Edwin Weekes are absent at work in the harvest fields making bonds. Samuel Baker is absent for a similar reason.

4th October 1885	Rose and Arthur Lower, Susannah and William Baker ... returned from the Hop Gardens.
26th June 1886	Mr Burton of Berwick Court has been employing several boys who ought to be in regular attendance at School.
11th October 1886	Rose Lower returned to school after an absence of sixteen weeks.
25th June 1889	John Button and James Button being employed haymaking.
1st July 1894	The children absent last week pulling weeds on Mr Champion's land ... have returned to school today.
28th October 1898	I have drawn the attention of the Board to the several cases of elder children who in anticipation of their attaining 13 years of age commenced attending badly two or three months before their birthday.
6th October 1899	The attendance owing to Blackberrying and other causes has been very poor throughout the week.
18th April 1902	Several girls have attended badly during the past week. 'Spring Cleaning' is the general excuse.

Some pupils, of course, took the legal way out, submitting themselves for Labour Certificates which enabled them to leave school early. The Labour Certificate was granted after successfully passing an examination at Standard III or Standard IV level.

13th April 1894	The following children scheduled for Labour Certificates, having passed, have left school: Burgess, Fred; Davis, Rose; Norman, Jesse; Weekes, Alice; Lelliott, Elizabeth.

15th March 1897	Received schedule of children examined for Labour Certificate. All the children entered viz. Albert Foord, William Bristow, Jos Lockwood, Emily Marchant, Alice Baker, have passed.
4th June 1901	Elsie Baker, Edwd Burgess, Frank Baker and Fred Marchant examined and passed for Labour Certificates.
30th June 1902	C Harman, L Norman and Daisy Davis examined and passed for Labour Certificate.

Pages 36 to 39

It is not unlikely that the parents of the children whose work is illustrated here signed their names with a cross. The children whose work is represented - W K Aikman, G Fannie Pemberton and Alice Knott - were not pupils at Alfriston.

Vere Foster's Copy Books were popular throughout the country and used at Alfriston School.

One of the examples shows how children learnt to form their letters.

Edinburgh Collegiate School,
10th October, 1890.

Dear Sir,

I was very agreeably surprised to find that I had gained the First Prize in Writing. Next year I intend to compete in Painting, and I shall do my utmost to succeed.

With warmest thanks for your handsome award,

I remain, yours very truly,
W. K. Aikman.

Vere Foster, Esq.

Edinburgh Collegiate School
10th October, 1890

Dear Sir,

I was very agreeably surprised to find that I had gained the First Prize in Writing. Next year I intend to compete in Painting, and I shall do my utmost to succeed.

With warmest thanks for your handsome award,

I remain, yours very truly,
W. K. Aikman

Vere Foster, Esq.

Alice Arnott   August 3, 1894

Boys

I do not like boys. They are so rough and
noisy. They think them-selves much
cleverer than girls but they are mistaken.
Girls are much more useful to their mothers
than boys. If you see a boy nursing a
baby he does it so clumsily you think
all the time he is going to let it drop.
Boys make their sisters do all sorts of things
such as clean their boots, brush their clothes,
put their playthings-bats, balls, bats,
and marbles safely away. When a boy
has tooth-ache he makes a deal more fuss about
it than a girl would, and mother to do a deal
of things to make him quiet, then boys
are so fond of play that they cannot
find time to come for their meals and
if they are not ready just when they
want them make a row about it. The best
thing to do then is to let them go without,
and you may be sure that they will come
to the bread and butter, before the bread

and butter will go to them. It costs
more to keep boys than girls they wear out
their boots so quickly and tear their clothes
so dreadfully that the shoemaker and tailor
are always calling at the house. Girls do
not wear out half so many cloths.
Folks say girls talk more than boys, but
you should hear them at ball or marbles
and then you would not think so. Etc.
I suppose there must be boys or we
should have no one to work horses, sweep
horses, plough the fields, look after gardens
and shops. The nicest boy I know is Willie
Murphy, he is a very nice fellow.

Scripture

1. What is the meaning of the word Exodus.

1. The word Exodus derives its name from the principal event recorded in it, namely the departure of the Israelites from the land of Egypt which in the Greek Septuagint translation is expressed by the word exodos that is a going out.

2. Why is the book of Leviticus so called,

2. The book of Leviticus is so called from its containing the regulations relative to the priests, Levities and sacrifices.

3. By whom is it supposed the last eight verses of the book of Deuteronomy were written,

3. They are supposed to have been written by Joshua, Samuel, and Esdras.

4. Why is the book of Numbers so called,

4. It is called from the circumstance that it contains the numbers and classification of the Hebrews and Levities after the erection and consecration of the tabernacle.

W W W W W W W W W
W W W W W W W W W W
X X X X X X X X X X
X X X X X X X X X X

Wanderer Wanderer Wanderer
Wanderer Wanderer Wanderer
Xerodes Xerodes Xerodes
Xerodes Xerodes Xerodes

Little	brooks	make	great	rivers
Little	brooks	make	great	rivers

4. FEES

The provision of universal popular education was an enormous undertaking even for a country which prided itself as the workshop of the world, the wealthiest nation there had ever been. The burden of payment for education had until 1878 been borne by the Church and other voluntary agencies. Now, it was to be picked up by the State. But not without some contribution by those who were intended to benefit. School fees, usually on a sliding scale, determined by the individual School Boards, were collected weekly.

Not unnaturally these fees were resented by many, resisted and avoided by others. The Log Book and Minute Books are littered with references to the difficulties of collection. In 1891, fee paying came to an end.

4th June 1879	Commenced school with bad attendance, many parents keeping children at home to avoid paying school fees.
27th October 1879	At the meeting of the Board in the evening it was decided to raise the Standard of School Fees from 1d to 2d as paid hitherto to the rates of 2d, 3d, and 6d .... Labourers to pay 2d for each child, Journeymen, tradesmen 3d each child and Mastermen 6d each child.
5th May 1880	Gave notice on 3rd inst that the School Fees would be raised in each Child's case 1d of which is to be returned to the Children on Condition of Regular and Punctual Attendance.
10th May 1880	Several attended bringing the money they had previously paid and not the raised fee.

29th November 1880	At a meeting of the Board on Saturday it was decided that the extra 1d brought by the children should be discontinued.
24th June 1882	Resolved that Thomas Marchant, Hy Baker, David Taylor, Chas Reed and G Streekly have notice served them, that if the arrears are not paid and School attendances amended they will be summoned.
10th December 1883	William Norman refused admission this morning, he having presented himself without his school fee.
8th February 1884	On Monday last Clara Reed brought to School a bad penny as one penny of her school fee. Her mother has not returned a good one.
12th October 1885	Frank Russell, Rose Lower, Arthur Lower, William Nye and Caroline Nye, all from Winton, presented themselves without their Fee and were refused admission.
21st December 1886	Received 5/- from the Relieving Officer as School fees for the six pauper children on the Registers for the quarter ended September 28th.

29th January 1887

Tradesmen (not journeymen) and Farmers first child	4d per week
every member of the same family	4d " "
Mechanics First Child	4d " "
every member of the same family	3d " "
Labourers including Working Foremen, each child	2d " "

41

3rd December 1887	Mrs William Russell of Winton Street attended before the Board and applied for a remission of School Fees stating that she had six in family and out of these 4 attended School, that her husband was a general labourer earning 12/- per week less 1/6 for rent and one boy earned 5/- per week.

Resolved that the School fees for the 2 youngest children be remitted for a period of two months.

(School Board Minute Book)

28th September 1889	Mrs Carter, the wife of Henry Thomas Carter, attended before the Board and thanked them for remitting the School Fees of her children ... Mrs Carter stated that her husband was now in receipt of 14/- per week and two boys out at work, one earning 5/- and the other 5/6 and 6 attending school one of which she had paid for and the other five had been remitted.

The Board resolved to remit for a period of 3 months the fees payable in respect of the three elder children on condition that the parent pays the fees for the three youngest and that the whole of them attend school.

(School Board Minute Book)

14th April 1890	Alice Baker not bringing the weekly fee (4d) as directed by the Board was sent home.
5th May 1890	Again refused attendance of Alice Baker, her parents sending only 2d as School Fees.

29th March 1890   Mrs Cottrell attended and complained of the
                         Fee of 4d charged for her child and
                         compared with a fee of 2d paid by others
                         whom she considered are in a position equal
                         to her husband.
                                        (School Board Minute Book)

14th September 1891 No schools fees have been collected ... the
                     Managers having accepted the Fee Grant.

Pages 45 to 46

Object lessons presented children with a broad though elementary introduction to science.

The dialogue 'Wood' from 'Forest, Field and Garden' reminds us of how much chanting of poems, tables, facts went on in classrooms at the time.

Object Lessons in Botany : From Forest field and Garden : Book I by E. SNELGROVE 1894

V.

ORANGES.

(THE GOLDEN APPLES OF THE HESPERIDES.)

Oranges, candied peel, oil of orange, dried orange peel.

ABOUT ORANGES GENERALLY.

1. Show an orange to the class. Ask a few questions about the sweet taste of oranges, where they grow, and the different kinds. Add to what they know.

    (a) Oranges grow in warm countries.

    (b) They are brought to us chiefly from Spain and the West Indies.

    (c) Oranges will not ripen in England except in an orange or hot house.

2. Tell of or show some of the different kinds.

    (a) Seville oranges (Spain)—bitter.

    (b) St. Michael   ,,   —sweet.

    (c) Maltese (Malta)—red inside.

    (d) Jaffa (Palestine)—large.

THE OUTSIDE OF AN ORANGE.

Question on the external characters, and so get from the children :—

    (a) An orange is globular in shape and of about the size of an apple.

    (b) It is soft and smooth to the touch.

    (c) Its surface is full of little holes.

    (d) It has a very pleasant odour.

THE INSIDE.

1. Cut an orange through the middle horizontally and show the arrangement of the parts. Question the children as to what these parts are :—

    (a) It consists of a thick peel or rind and a juicy pulp.

    (b) In the pulp there are *pips* or *seeds*.

    (c) The pulp is divided into 8 or 10 parts.

    (d) These parts are broad towards the outside and narrow in the middle of the orange.

V.—SUMMARY.

MATTER.—Timber is obtained from large forests. Imported and carried in barges. Stacked in timber-yard and sold by timber merchant.

METHOD.—Briefly recapitulate the points of the lesson, and refer to timber-yard where wood is stored and sold.

DIALOGUE—"WOOD."

Teacher:

Wood is obtained from mighty old trees;
Can you give me the English names of these?

Children:

The lime and the oak, the beech and the elm,
The fir and the birch, are the best in the realm.

Teacher:

Who brings them from forest or woodland glen?

Children:

The lumberer with his gang of men,
With saw and axe they hew them down,
And send the best to London Town.

Teacher:

But how are these big trees brought to town?

Children:

They are carried on rafts and floated down
Canals or rivers along with the breeze,
Till they stop at the wharf and are shipped with ease.

Teacher:

A raft! What is that? Pray how does it carry
The largest of trees? It surely must tarry.

Children:

A raft is made of trees linked together
Upon which people live in all kinds of weather;
It is like a flat floor all covered with trees,
Which floats down the stream till it comes to the sea.

Teacher:

Who makes the tree smooth from branches and leaves?

Children:

Why, the joiner; he planes and the edges he sheaves;
And then all the boards that he works upon so,
Are stacked by the timber merchants, you know,
The stoutest and strongest our ships for to make,
And houses and doors a quantity take.

5. SOME MISCELLANEOUS PURCHASES

Nowadays, head teachers have control over their budgets. So too did the Master of Alfriston School. The Log Book contains interminable lists of mundane items of the kind represented here.

20th November 1879   Received 2 cwt coal, 1 cwt coke.

19th January 1880   Received one box of nibs.

10th December 1880   Received 1 gross of copybooks and ½ a gross of dictation books, also ½ gallon of Ink.

23rd October 1881   Received 2 cwt coal from H Russell.

30th January 1883   Received 50 bundles of firewood of Mr Bodle.

12th February 1883   Received 6 reels of Cotton of Mr Comfort.

26th February 1883   Received 6 boxes of Matches of Mr Bodle.

19th March 1883   Received 8 reels of sewing cotton and 2 doz linen buttons of Mr Humphries.

7th April 1883   Received of Messrs Blackie and Sons.

3 dozen poetry books for Repetition Standards 1 and 2

1½ do   do   Standard 3

5 3/4 doz grammars for all Standards

30th May 1884   Received 2 Osborne desks from the National Society and 1 gall ink.

18th April 1883	Received of the National Society's Depot
	1 Master's Desk, 1 Stool, Pictures of Turkey, Sturgeon, Jackal, Walrus, Common Whale, Newfoundland Dog, Rook, Common Seal, Hare, Mouse, Toad and Rabbit.
5th June 1889	Received from the Sanitary Inspector
	2 Packets and 1 Bottle of Disinfectant.
9th September 1889	Resumed school after five weeks holiday. The school and offices have been cleaned during the vacation and the following articles from Mr Bodle used for the purpose:
	2 yds Flannel 1/-; Soap -/5; Extract Soap -/3; Blk Lead 1½; Pail 1/-.
1st March 1890	Received from the National Society
	3 boxes Slate Pencils 1 Quire Blotting Paper
13th November 1895	Received parcel of 63 books from Mr J Pulsford, Eastbourne. These books are for distribution among the children as prizes for conduct and attendance.

Needlework was an important feature of the timetable. Large numbers of girls went into service and it was essential that they were appropriately equipped for this work.

The sampler comes from 'The Standard Needlework Book'.

Drill was the precursor of modern physical education. It was highly formalised and its name suggests how it was carried out. The extract is from 'Infants School Drill'.

A MARKING SAMPLER.
SEE FOURTH STANDARD.
WIDTH: A hundred stitches (requiring two hundred threads).

LENGTH: A hundred and twenty-nine stitches (requiring two hundred and fifty-eight threads.)

One space on the printed Sampler represents TWO threads EACH WAY on the Canvas (the number taken for a Cross-stitch).
An Eyelet-hole stitch requires FOUR threads EACH WAY (See the Capitals in the Name).

In the small Alphabet V and W can, if preferred, be made like the Capital letters and the Y like that in " Mary." The Canvas should be cut with a margin of two inches and longer than the Pattern if more space is wanted for the Name and Date.

INFANTS' SCHOOL DRILL.

POSITION.

N the first place the children must be made to stand in rows at arm's length from each other (see fig. 1), and each row must be an arm's length apart (see fig. 2), in order to leave sufficient room for the thorough accomplishment of every exercise. Chalk lines, or rows of chalked marks, may be made on the floor to secure regularity ; but it has been found a better plan to have brass nails permanently put into the floor, for the children to know at once where to place themselves for drill.

The children must then be made to stand in a particular position, and they must resume that position after the completion of any exercise.

In this position, the heels must be together ; the toes turned out (not too much) ; the head held erect ; the hands resting on the hips, with the fingers in front and the thumbs behind ; the shoulders thrown well back ; the chest expanded ; and the body in an upright position (see fig. 3).

It will be found necessary to remind the children of these particulars after nearly every movement, and to make them return to their marked places.

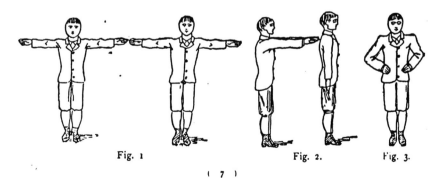

Fig. 1   Fig. 2.   Fig. 3.

6. BUILDINGS, FURNITURE, EQUIPMENT

When Mr Dance took up his post in June 1879, the Board agreed that the house, which the Master was to occupy rent free, should be "put in repair, papered and painted and the Board agreed to advance the sum of £25 for the purchase of furniture."

An inventory of furniture provided for the Master included "1 Round Kitchen Table, 4 cane seated chairs, 2 arm chairs, 2 bedroom chairs, 1 card table, 1 wooden bedstead, 1 small feather bed, 1 full sized mattress, 1 dressing table, 1 wash stand, 1 small looking glass".

The Board, conscious of the shortcomings of the house, gave Mr Dance an allowance of three shillings a week for laundry "until the Board can afford better accommodation". A new door and porch were to be added.

In spite of these efforts, in 1881, Her Majesty's Inspectors stated that "The Teacher's residence is a very poor one and should if possible be improved and proper Office accommodation provided for him". There is perhaps an ambiguity here: I am confident that in this context 'Office' means lavatory.

John Wilson was called in 1882 to put in a sink and a ten gallon copper in the house. We may assume that this latter was for laundry purposes and that the three shilling allowance was then withdrawn.

If the house was in poor condition, then so throughout many years was the school. Over time, new furniture and equipment were purchased but always there were complaints about the basic fabric of the school. As much as anything, it was the "offices" which made life unpleasant. At the back of the building, there appears to have been a partitioned 'office', one side for girls, the other for boys. The cesspool stunk at all seasons.

21st March 1879	The present state of school offices causes great inconvenience and tends to produce anything but a good effect upon children's morals. The close proximity of the school, too, is bad in a sanitary point of view.

10th October 1879   I have again found the closets a great nuisance this week being obliged to close the door and windows to keep back the stench.

In April 1881, Her Majesty's Inspector writes: "The children's offices cannot be accepted".

19th February 1886   Received two bottles of Chloride of Lime for use in the Offices.

In August 1887 the Board resolved "that a shaft be put up to carry away the effluvia from the closets after they have been cleaned out".

9th March 1889   The School Rooms and Offices have been thoroughly cleaned and the following articles from Mr Bodle have been used for the purpose:-

2 Yards House Flannel	
2 Scrubbing Brushes	1/-
Soap	6d
Black Lead	3d
Extract of Soap	3d

The offices continued to be a problem. In February 1891, the Inspector of Nuisances to the Rural Sanitary Authority of Eastbourne required the Board within the month "... to abate an alleged nuisance at the School premises and for that purpose to do away with the existing cesspool for closets". What was required, he said, was either earth or ash closets.

An Architect's report in 1901 states: "There are no proper latrines at present ... Proper latrines with water supply and drains or a proper system of Earth closets having compulsory frequent use of Deodorising material should be used".

And so it continued.

There had always been the potential for dispute between the Board and the Church which owned the School building. Until the arrival of the Reverend F W Beynon in 1889, however, both parties had been on the warmest terms. In the nine years of Mr Beynon's stay there was a series of small squabbles.

In 1890, the Board decided to erect a porch, with lavatories at each end and with pegs for clothing. Mr Pinyoun records his delight in the Log Book.

1st November 1890   A great improvement has been made to the school. A porch of corrugated iron has been erected and will be furnished with lavatories, hat pegs, etc.

A fortnight later his cheerfulness has evaporated.

14th November 1890   The Porch above referred to has been removed. This, I believe, is owing to an objection raised by the Vicar.

This particular struggle between the Board and the Vicar went on for another three years. How the members of the Board must have regretted the departure of his predecessors. Solicitors' letters were exchanged; alternative plans offered and rejected; on at least one occasion the Vicar refused to meet the Board members. In 1893 a new corrugated iron porch was put up, but it was torn down and the sheets sold for 1/- each. However, the matter was eventually resolved and two porches with coat pegs were erected: the plan to have a lavatory at each end was abandoned.

Miss Jenner, writing in 'Cuckmere News' in December 1990, says that "These were just lean-to lobbies, three walls and a roof, each side of the main entrance .... The old brick path served as a floor, but the children still had to walk along the now narrowed path to reach the privies at the back of the hall."

The inventory of school furniture inherited from the National School, lists in 1883:

"10 Windsor desks, 42 Windsor inkwells, Maps of Europe, Africa, Asia, Master's desk with table, Harmonium, 3 Chairs,

Classroom stove, Clock, 2 Small Easels, 4 Blackboards, 6 Forms, 1 Form with back, 1 Work Table, 1 Card Stand, 1 Bell, 1 Abacus."

The Board subsequently bought:
"3 large Osborne desks, 2 small ditto, 2 infants ditto, 24 Osborne inkwells, 1 master's inkwell, 1 large Easel, maps of England, Ireland, Scotland, the World, Sussex, chart of Geographical definitions, Stove in large room, infants gallery."

The infants' gallery was a form of raked seating. Miss Jenner describes them as "a tier of wooden steps, where the infants had to sit at the mercy of the feet of those above them." The gallery was in use for concerts long after the school had decamped to North Road.

Since the school opened there had been complaints about the furniture.

8th March 1879   The desks at present in use (old Windsor) prove very awkward, especially to the girls and smaller children, stepping over the seats being necessary to getting in and out. Furniture of school generally is very primitive.

Nevertheless, these old six seater desks were used over seventy years later as supplementary seating when the building, no longer a school, was used for concerts and plays.

Two years later, the Inspector's report commented: "The benches in the Infant room are unsuitable. They should be low enough for the little ones' feet to rest on the floor. Another window is needed in this room, and then the Gallery should be placed at the end opposite to the entrances to the principal room ..."

An Inspector's report, in 1887 states:

"Some of the (infant) benches are ill-adapted to their purpose and should be removed and replaced by a few modern Infant Desks."

55

Yet another report in 1895 says:

"The furniture and appliances are not of the best."

But there was a miscellany of complaints recorded over the years. For instance, the stoves did not always work.

21st November 1879   I must here call attention to the fact that there is no means of lighting a fire in the large room.

5th December 1879   The children have all worked together since the cold weather set in in the Infants Room although little could be done for want of space.

20th October 1905   The conditions of the stoves in the Infants Room need attention: fires cannot at present be lighted in them.

Sometimes it was impossible for the children to do any work.

26th November 1883   At the Board Meeting held on Saturday last, application was made for Lamps for the purpose of lighting the School during the dark afternoons of the Winter Months. The application was refused.

Sometimes there were anxieties about health hazards.

25th June 1886   The following is the report of Dr Fussell upon the quality of water in the well in front of the house:

'Of fair average drinking quality. By proper filtration (which I should always use if obliged to drink it) it would become a 1st class water for drinking purposes.'

Later in the year, Mr Greey reported to the Board that there was plenty of good water in the well and that he used it for domestic purposes. In later years, after the school had moved to North Road, boys and girls playing on the Tye often quenched their thirst at this old well.

After children had negotiated the often muddy lanes and paths, they frequently had to struggle across the Tye.

13th November 1882   The Path leading across the Tye is in such a wretched condition that some parents will not send their children to school.

Mr Dance had suggested two years earlier that the path should be paved or asphalted. His suggestion was taken up in 1965.

By 1903, the Inspector writes: "It will not be possible for me to recommend much longer a recognition of these premises as efficient."

15th June 1903   The Infants have today been transferred temporarily to the Assembly Room of 'The Star'.

20th June 1903   The rain comes into the School Room through the roof in several places.

They held out, teachers and pupils, until 1908.

On the day the school on the Tye closed, Mr Pinyoun is extraordinarily reticent. He writes:

31st July 1908   Closed School for Summer vacation. Alice Taylor resigned her post as Monitress in Infants Division.

It is said, however, that on the day they took over the North Road School, the pupils, some wearing red sashes, marched with their teachers from the Tye to the new premises. It was, one supposes, a kind of triumph.

The present school in North Road has its beginnings in that school on the Tye. And there is a debt due to that original school, to its dedicated School Board members, to its earnest Masters and other teachers and to those hundreds of children who, willingly or no, were the first of their blood to have full-time education. In the first thirty years or so, the curriculum altered beyond what the legislators had ever dreamt of: that in itself is an acknowledgement that this village, like others throughout the land, was not willing simply to accept the narrow diet of learning prescribed by a remote Government.

The story of Alfriston School cannot be told in its entirety. The evidence is too slight and documents are too sparse. But I hope that from what is available, I have provided some idea of how the school on the Tye developed and that I have, if only briefly, introduced some of those who were involved in that development.

7. APPENDICES

i) The Law

Bylaws under Section 74 of the Elementary Education Act, 1870, as amended by the Elementary Education Act of 1876 for the United School District of Alfriston.

"2. The parent of every child not less than 5, nor more than 13 years of age, shall cause such child to attend school, unless there be a reasonable excuse for non-attendance.

5. (a) A child between ten and thirteen years of age shall not be required to attend school if such child has received a certificate from one of Her Majesty's Inspectors of Schools that it has reached the Fourth Standard prescribed by the Code of 1876.

(b) A child between ten and thirteen shown to the satisfaction of the Local Authority to be beneficially and necessarily employed shall not be required to attend School for more than 150 attendances each year if such child has received a certificate from one of Her Majesty's Inspectors of Schools that it has reached the Third Standard prescribed by the Code of 1876."

In 1889 the school leaving age was raised to fourteen but with exemptions for those employed part-time in factories or in agriculture from the age of eleven. Many Alfriston parents took advantage of this.

Those children who were under ten or those who could not be exempted because of their failure to reach Standard III or IV were expected to complete at least two hundred attendances. A full day's attendance counted as two attendances.

Pupils who attended two hundred and fifty times a year for five years were allowed to leave school without reaching Standard III.

ii) The Teaching Staff

The school on the Tye had four Masters in the years from 1879 to 1908. Each was assisted by either his sister or his wife who was generally responsible for needlework and the infants class. The Masters' salaries ranged from £100 to £140 a year.

The Masters and their Assistants were:

February 1879 - June 1879	Mr W T Brown and Miss K E Brown
June 1879 - April 1880	Mr E J Dance and Mrs C Dance
April 1880 - June 1888	Mr H B Greey and Miss E Greey
June 1888 - July 1908	Mr W Pinyoun and Mrs E Pinyoun (née Miss E Harman)

Mr and Mrs Pinyoun transferred to the Primary School in North Road in 1908.

During the period there were other Assistant Teachers as the school had for most of the time well over a hundred children on roll. At one point there were one hundred and sixty children in attendance. Among those Assistants were Misses Cox, Dance (later Mrs Pratt), Riding, Melling, Cutler, Sheen, White, Pearson, Lerwill, Hildred, Wighton. No blame can attach to the school for the fleeting nature of some of the appointments; young women often found it difficult to assimilate into closed village communities.

Other Assistants were Mr Jesse Comfort and Eunice Dumbrell, both of whom had been pupils at the school and had in turn been monitors and then pupil teachers.

Thirteen and fourteen year olds were often appointed as monitors to give basic instruction to younger children. Some of them worked in that capacity for two or three years, earning one or two shillings each week. These included Frederick Bodle, Rose Russell, Rosina Shelley, the Comforts - Jesse, Walter and Ebenezer junior - Mary Turner, Lydia Taylor, Alice Taylor.

Among those promoted to pupil teacher at about £10 a year were Rose Pickard and Fanny Weekes. Poor lame Frederick Bodle has been mentioned earlier. Pupil teachers taught up to six hours a week, took regular examinations and were given special instruction by the Master. After five years they could go to Teacher Training

College or be appointed as a full-time assistant teacher of unqualified status. In July 1888, Mr Pinyoun records buying books for Jesse Comfort, the pupil teacher. These were "1 Grammar; 1 Algebra; 1 Geography; 1 Arithmetic; 1 Latin Grammar; 1 History". Two years later Jesse was to receive a copy of Gladman's 'School Management'.

iii)The Teaching Organisation

There were over the years anything from forty to sixty infants on roll and at one stage about ninety pupils in what was known as the mixed class where ages ranged from seven to twelve or thirteen.

Usually the infants were taught by the Master's wife who might be assisted by a monitor. This was not always the case.

Mr Greey writing in the Log Book on 10th September 1886 sounds distinctly weary:

"I have devoted nearly the whole of the week to the Infants ... the class is a very large one (50), almost too large for one teacher to manage satisfactorily."

In 1903, the Inspector's report is sympathetic to Mr Pinyoun managing Standards Three to Seven which might have numbered sixty pupils.

The infants, in their galleried seats, were partitioned off from the mixed class which had pupils across a wide age range, of very different abilities and divided into Standards. The groups were set tasks thought appropriate to their needs and were supervised by the Master, who would flit from group to group, and would most frequently have an Assistant or a pupil teacher or a monitor to support him.

61

iv) The Code of Standards (1876)

Standard I

Reading:	Narrative in monosyllables.
Writing:	Form on blackboard or slate, from dictation, letters, capital and small manuscript.
Arithmetic:	Form on blackboard or slate, from dictation, figures up to 20; name at sign figures up to 20; add and subtract figures up to 10, orally, from example on blackboard.

Standard II

Reading:	One of the Narratives next in order after monosyllables in an elementary reading book used in the school.
Writing:	Copy in manuscript character a line of print.
Arithmetic:	A sum in simple addition or subtraction and the multiplication table.

Standard III

Reading:	A short paragraph from an elementary reading book used in the school.
Writing:	A sentence from the same paragraph, slowly read once, and then dictated in simple words.
Arithmetic:	A sum in any simple rule as far as short division.

Standard IV

Reading:	A short paragraph from a more advanced reading book used in the school.
Writing:	A sentence slowly dictated once by a few words at a time from the same book, but not from the paragraph read.
Arithmetic:	A sum in compound rules (money).

Standard V

Reading:	A few lines of poetry from a reading book used in the first class of the school.
Writing:	A sentence slowly dictated once by a few words at a time.
Arithmetic:	A sum in compound rules (common weights and measures).

Standard VI

Reading:	A short ordinary paragraph in a newspaper or other modern narrative.
Writing:	Another short ordinary paragraph in a newspaper or other modern narrative, slowly dictated once, by a few words at a time.
Arithmetic:	A sum in practice or bills of parcels.

In 1882 an additional standard was added for thirteen year olds.

BIBLIOGRAPHY

Primary Sources
Log Book   Alfriston School, 1879 - 1908
Minute Books   Alfriston United School Board, 1879 - 1903
Minute Book   Guardians of the Poor, Eastbourne Union, 1880

By far the greatest number of quotes in this account comes from the Log Book. The synopses of the reports of the Inspectors appear there also. It must have been a chastening experience for the Master to have to record sometimes adverse criticism. The Members of the Board were active enough and powerful enough to ensure that the full sense of what the Inspectors had highlighted, was accurately represented in the Log Book.

The passages I have taken from the School Board Minute Book are acknowledged in the text.

Secondary Sources
A History of Alfriston, F A Pagden, 1924
Alfriston, A Cecil Piper, 1970
Alfriston, R M Boyd, 1989
Cuckmere News, J Jenner, November/December, 1990
Morning has Broken: Pirton School, Joan Wayne, 1987
Payment by Results: Uckfield Parochial School, Simon Wright, 1991

ORIGINAL SOURCE MATERIAL
Reading Without Tears, 1861
A Standard Needlework Book, 1874
The Advanced Excelsior, Book V, 1877
Infants' School Drill, 1887
Vere Foster's Copy Books, c. 1890
Forest, Field and Garden: Book I, 1894

The above books are typical of the time. It is not clear in every case who printed or published each of them.

Vere Foster's books for the training of handwriting skills were certainly used at Alfriston.

The written work of three pupils is included. None of these attended Alfriston School.

By the same author